SLAMET RIYADI, DR. HJ. RODHATUL JENNA

Practical Guide to IT-Based Instructional Media Development

For Islamic Education

First published by Asadel Publisher 2024

Copyright © 2024 by Slamet Riyadi, Dr. Hj. Rodhatul Jenna

All rights reserved. No part of this publication may be reproduced, stored or transmitted in any form or by any means, electronic, mechanical, photocopying, recording, scanning, or otherwise without written permission from the publisher. It is illegal to copy this book, post it to a website, or distribute it by any other means without permission.

First edition

This book was professionally typeset on Reedsy.
Find out more at reedsy.com

Contents

Foreword	v
TOOLS AND MATERIALS	1
PRACTICUM MODULE 1 (ANIMAKER)	2
SUBJECT	2
LEARNING OBJECTIVES	2
BASIC THEORY	3
ANIMAKER	4
EVALUATION	6
PRACTICUM MODULE 2 (CHARACTER)	8
SUBJECT	8
LEARNING OBJECTIVES	8
BASIC THEORY	8
TEST	9
EVALUATION	17
PRACTICUM MODULE 3 (SHAPES)	19
SUBJECT	19
LEARNING OBJECTIVES	19
BASIC THEORY	19
TEST	20
EVALUATION	25
PRACTICUM MODULE 4 (TEXT)	26
SUBJECT	26
LEARNING OBJECTIVES	26
DESCRIPTION	26
TEST	27
EVALUATION	30

Add text to your project	30
PRACTICUM MODULE 5 (BACKGROUND)	31
SUBJECT	31
LEARNING OBJECTIVES	31
BASIC THEORY	31
TEST	32
EVALUATION	35
PRACTICUM MODULE 6 (IMAGE, VIDEO, MUSIC)	36
SUBJECT	36
LEARNING OBJECTIVES	36
BASIC THEORY	37
TEST	37
EVALUATION	40
PRACTICUM MODULE 7 (UPLOAD MENU)	42
SUBJECT	42
LEARNING OBJECTIVES	42
DESCRIPTION	42
TEST	43
EVALUATION	44
PRACTICUM MODULE 8 (SCENE AND TIMELINE)	45
SUBJECT	45
LEARNING OBJECTIVES	45
BASIC THEORY	45
TEST	46
EVALUATION	50
PRACTICUM MODULE 9 (RENDERING)	51
SUBJECT	51
LEARNING OBJECTIVES	51
BASIC THEORY	51
TEST	53
EVALUATION AND FINAL PROJECT	55
BIBLIOGRAPHY	56
ABOUT THE AUTHORS	57

Foreword

The author prays Praise and Gratitude to the presence of Allah SWT. Because of the abundance of His grace, the author was able to complete the practicum module for creating IT-based learning media in the PAI study program, Faculty of Tarbiyah and Teaching Sciences IAIN Palangka Raya.

This module contains detailed steps in the process of creating 2-dimensional animated learning media. This module is one of the modules prepared with the aim of being a practical learning medium for the IT-Based PAI Teaching Material Development course for the Islamic Religious Education (PAI) study program.

This module can be completed successfully thanks to support from various parties. The author realizes that there are still many shortcomings in the preparation of this module. Therefore, the author really hopes for criticism and suggestions for the improvement and perfection of this module.

Palangka Raya, 24 Juni 2024

signed

Writer

TOOLS AND MATERIALS

The tools and materials used in this practicum are:

1. Laptop or cellphone device, you can use just one
2. Stable internet connection
3. Internet Browser Software installed on your cellphone/laptop

PRACTICUM MODULE 1 (ANIMAKER)

SUBJECT

- Animation Learning Media

- Animaker Software

LEARNING OBJECTIVES

- Students can understand the meaning and examples of Animation Learning Media

- Students can open and create new projects in Animaker

BASIC THEORY

Media comes from Latin which is the plural form of "medium" which literally means intermediary or introduction. In general, it is anything that can channel information from the information source to the information recipient. The teaching and learning process is basically also a communication process, so basically the media used in learning is called learning media.

Definition of learning media according to experts:

1. According to Hairudin et al, they argue that "everything that can transmit information from the source to the recipient. As well as to achieve certain learning objectives that have been formulated."
2. According to the Big Indonesian Dictionary, "media are various types of components in a child's environment that can provide stimulation for learning".
3. According to Miarso, he believes that "learning media is anything that is used to convey messages and can stimulate the thoughts, feelings, attention and will of the learner so that it can encourage the learning process."
4. According to Dadan Djuanda, "Learning media is anything that can be used to channel messages from the sender to the recipient so that it can stimulate students' thoughts, feelings and attention so that the learning process occurs."

The definition of animation according to several experts, including:

1. According to Agus Suheri, the definition of animation is a collection of images that have been processed in such a way that they can produce movement.
2. According to Ibiz Fernandez, the definition of animation is a process of recording and playing back a series of static images to get the illusion of

movement.

ANIMAKER

Animaker is a software that provides software products for creating animated videos. Animaker provides both free and paid services. Animaker is animation creation software with an online process. In this application, the required background and characters are available.

The advantages of animaker are:

1. Can make learning more interesting and interactive.
2. Practical use.
3. Has interesting characters and animation.

The disadvantages of animaker are:

1. The manufacturing process must be connected to the internet.
2. Many features are paid.

CREATING A PROJECT IN ANIMAKER

PRACTICUM MODULE 1 (ANIMAKER)

Langkah-Langkahnya:

1. Siapkan Laptop yang terhubung dengan internet
2. Buka google menggunakan aplikasi web browser, disini saya menggunakan aplikasi google chrome.
3. Buka google menggunakan aplikasi web, karena disini saya terbiasa pakai chrome, maka toturialnya menggunakan aplikasi google chrome.
4. Pilih Animaker seperti yang dalam kotak merah

  Maka akan muncul tampilan seperti di atas, lalu klik Sign Up seperti pada gambar yang di lingkari merah.

PRACTICAL GUIDE TO IT-BASED INSTRUCTIONAL MEDIA DEVELOPMENT

⑥ Kemudian tampilan akan berubah seperti ini, di sini kita sebenarnya bisa Sign Up (mendaftar) dengan 3 cara: **Pertama** dengan E-mail, caranya dengan memasukkan User Name yang kita inginkan dan E-mail Address yang masih aktif, kemudian Password. Dan jangan lupa centang pada "I agree to all terms of service and privacy policy". terakhir Sign Up. Langkah berikutnya buka E-mail kita tadi, cari E-mail yang dikirim oleh Animaker. Lalu klik Link (tautan) yang diberikan, maka kita sudah terdaftar. **Kedua** dengan klik google, kita bisa dengan hanya mengklik google dan langsung terdaftar dengan catatan chrome kita sudah diaktifkan akun googlenya. **Ketiga** dengan Facebook, sama seperti google. kalau kita sudah pernah buka akun facebook di chrome dan password kita set auto-save. maka akan langsung terdaftar lewat akun facebook.

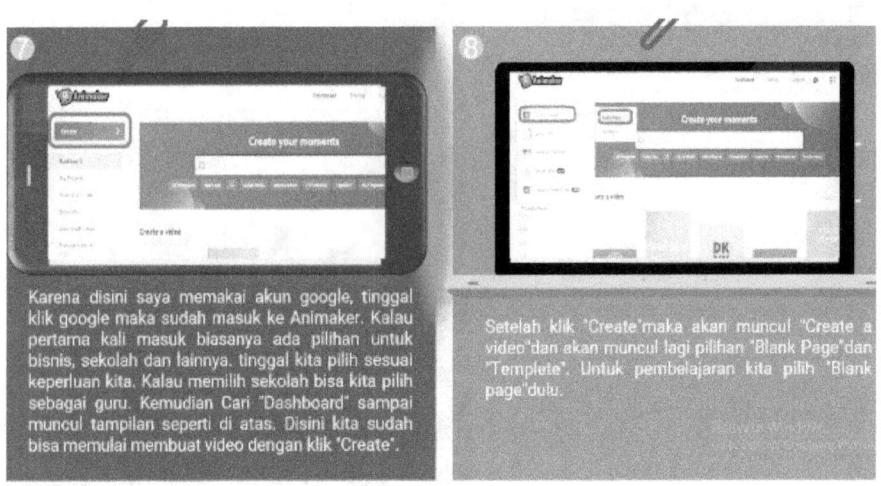

⑦ Karena disini saya memakai akun google, tinggal klik google maka sudah masuk ke Animaker. Kalau pertama kali masuk biasanya ada pilihan untuk bisnis, sekolah dan lainnya. tinggal kita pilih sesuai keperluan kita. Kalau memilih sekolah bisa kita pilih sebagai guru. Kemudian Cari "Dashboard" sampai muncul tampilan seperti di atas. Disini kita sudah bisa memulai membuat video dengan klik "Create".

⑧ Setelah klik "Create"maka akan muncul "Create a video"dan akan muncul lagi pilihan "Blank Page"dan "Templete". Untuk pembelajaran kita pilih "Blank page"dulu.

EVALUATION

1. What is meant by animated learning media
2. Register on the Animaker application (https://www.animaker.com)
3. Create an animated video project in Animaker with the name: **media_anmasi_nim_nam**

PRACTICUM MODULE 2 (CHARACTER)

SUBJECT

- Character

LEARNING OBJECTIVES

- Students can understand the function of characters in animation
- Students can determine appropriate characters for learning media

BASIC THEORY

PRACTICUM MODULE 2 (CHARACTER)

The definition of character in animation is generally the same as the definition of character in literary works, in that it has elements of narrative and visual depiction of a character. In the world of literature, according to Jones in Burhan, character is a form of depicting a clear picture of someone who is shown in a story.

Many of the characters present in animation use figures that represent humans or at least have human traits and characteristics, for example characters that basically do not physically represent humans, such as characters from animals, plants or inanimate objects.

TEST

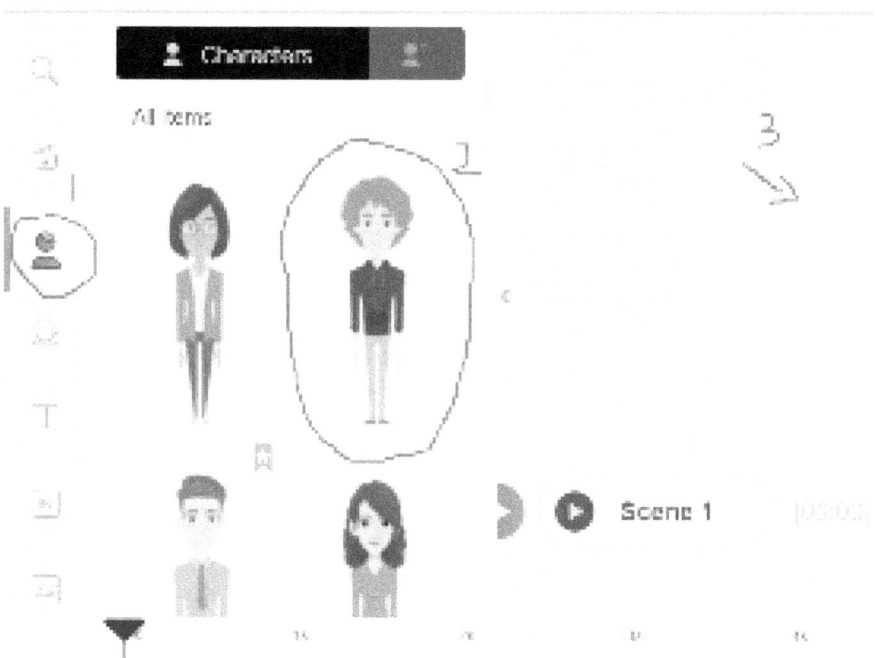

1. To add a character in Animaker, make sure the menu option is on the far left of the character menu. Then click on the desired character or drag the character to the white board.

Each character has Actions and Expressions. Actions are used to add action to a character, for example moving hands, walking, sitting, jumping, and so on. There are many choices of actions, both free and paid, according to your needs.

PRACTICUM MODULE 2 (CHARACTER)

1. Expression is used to change a character's facial expression. Select the Expression tab then there will be displayed many available expressions. For example, the expression is happy, sad, smiling, like, and so on. To select it, just click on the desired expression. The character's expression will change

To add voice to a character, click the microphone symbol next to the character. We can add sound by recording directly in Animaker, or through text that is converted into sound by Animaker, or by uploading a sound file that we already have

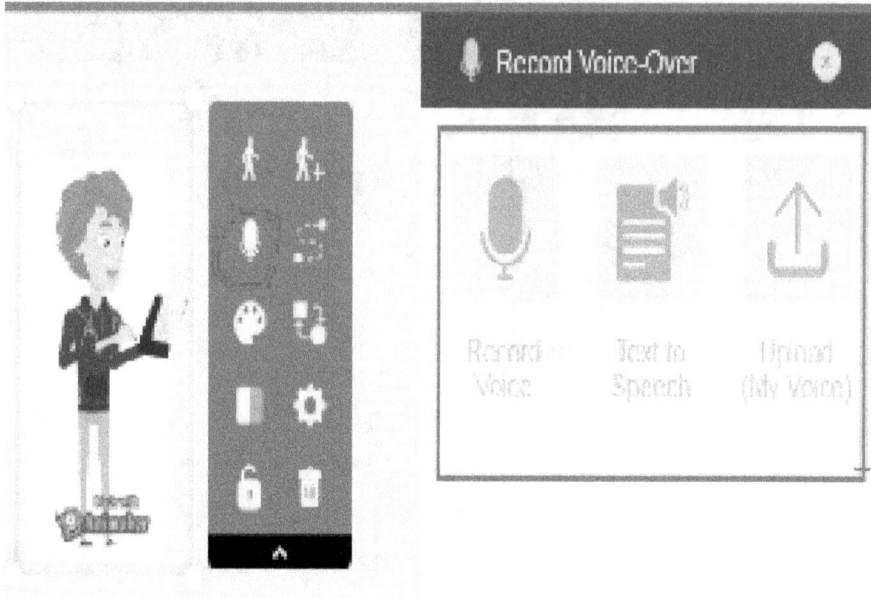

We can add moving movements to the characters. How to choose a smart move. Select the desired transfer model then click Apply

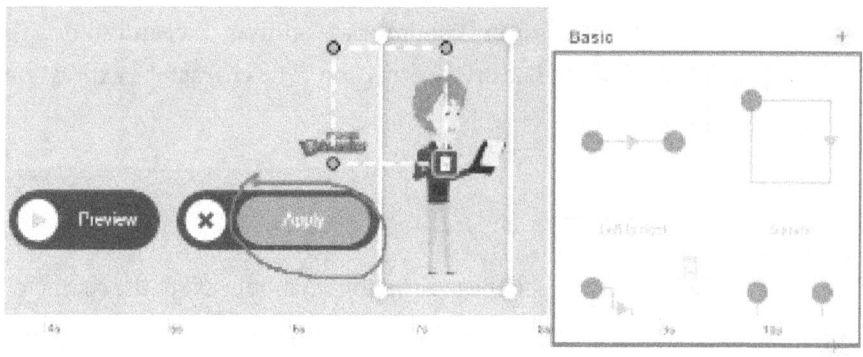

PRACTICUM MODULE 2 (CHARACTER)

We can change the color of the properties that the character has. You do this by clicking the change color symbol. We can change the color using custom themes or manually by changing one by one, such as eyes, skin, hair, etc

PRACTICAL GUIDE TO IT-BASED INSTRUCTIONAL MEDIA DEVELOPMENT

1.

PRACTICUM MODULE 2 (CHARACTER)

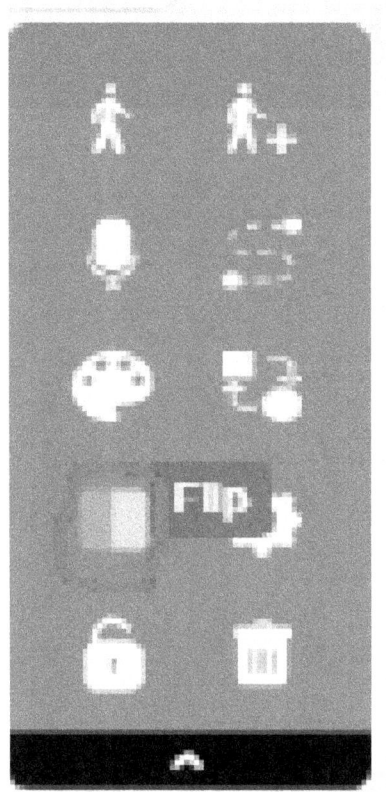 

1. Flip, this menu is used to change or reverse the character's position. For example, face right, face left, up and down
2. Settings, this menu is used to add enter effects (effects the first time the character is displayed), Exit effects (effects when the character has finished displaying), and Transparency (adjusts the transparency of the character

PRACTICAL GUIDE TO IT-BASED INSTRUCTIONAL MEDIA DEVELOPMENT

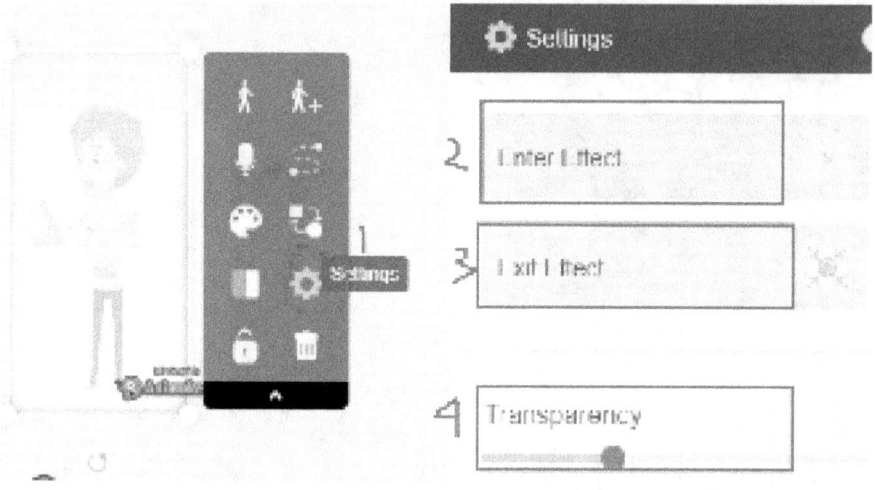

PRACTICUM MODULE 2 (CHARACTER)

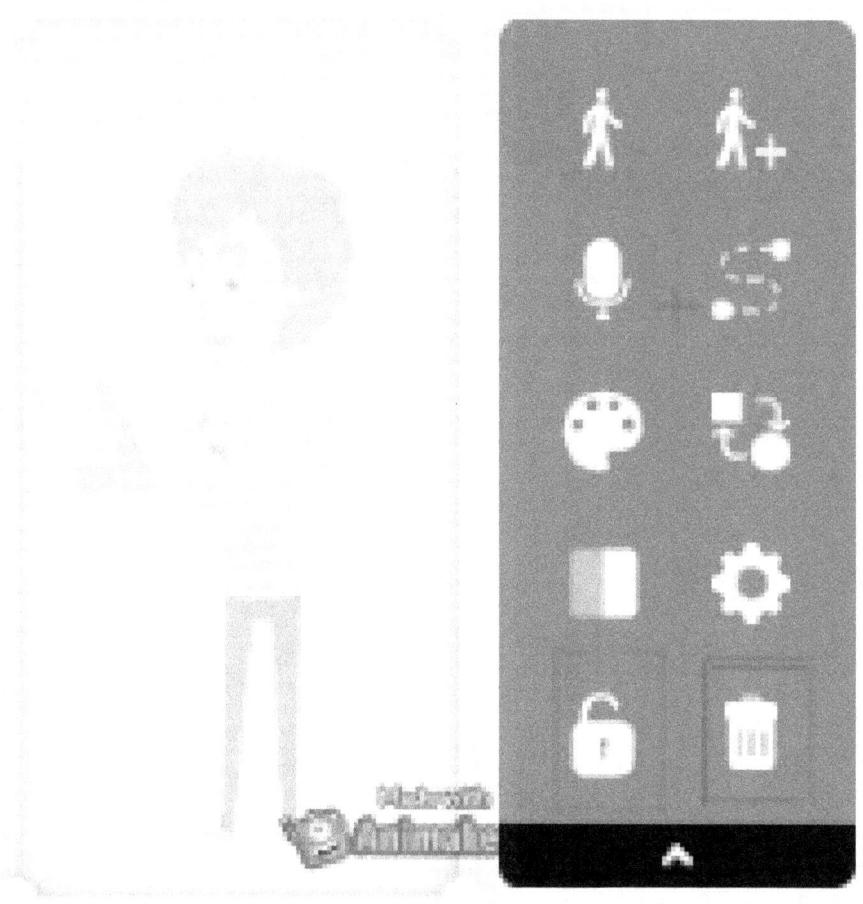

1. Lock, used to lock the Ahar character and cannot be changed anymore. Trash is used to delete these character

EVALUATION

1. What is a character in animation
2. Add a character to the project you have created, then change its properties, according to your own creation!

PRACTICUM MODULE 3 (SHAPES)

SUBJECT

- Shape (Shape)

LEARNING OBJECTIVES

- Students can know various shapes

- Students can add and manage shapes in animated videos

BASIC THEORY

PRACTICAL GUIDE TO IT-BASED INSTRUCTIONAL MEDIA DEVELOPMENT

The meaning of the word shape in the English – Indonesian Dictionary is kb. 1 shape. 2 pieces (of clothes, jewelry). 3 circumstances, conditions. -kkt. 1 form (st). 2 determine (o's future). -kki. shape up.

Shape is a meeting point between space and mass. Shape is also a geometric description of the part of the universe plane occupied by the object, which is determined by its outer boundaries but does not depend on its location (coordinates) and orientation (rotation) relative to the universal plane. occupied. The shape of the object also does not depend on specific properties such as: color, content, and material.

TEST

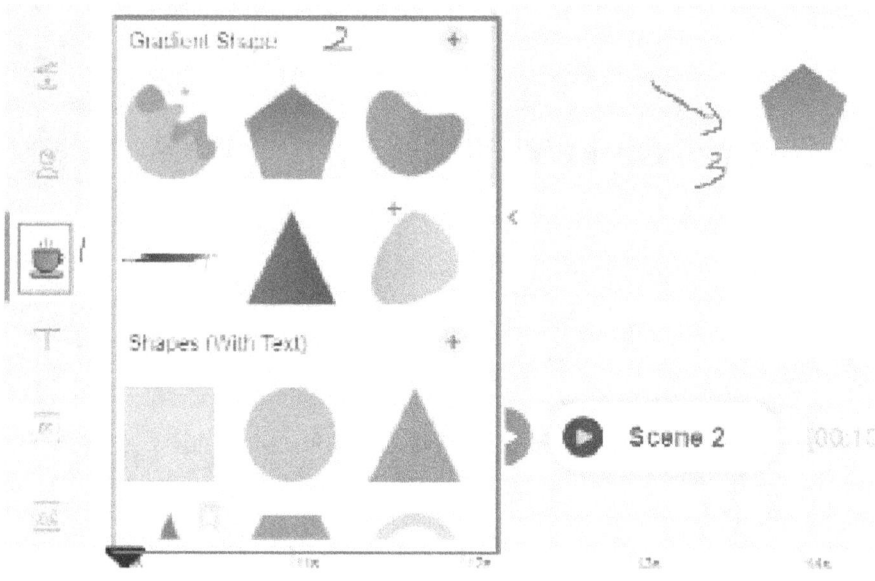

1. Select the shape menu with the coffee image, then click on the shape you want and it will automatically appear on the page.

2. We can add moving movements to the characters. How to choose a smart move. Select the desired transfer model then click Apply

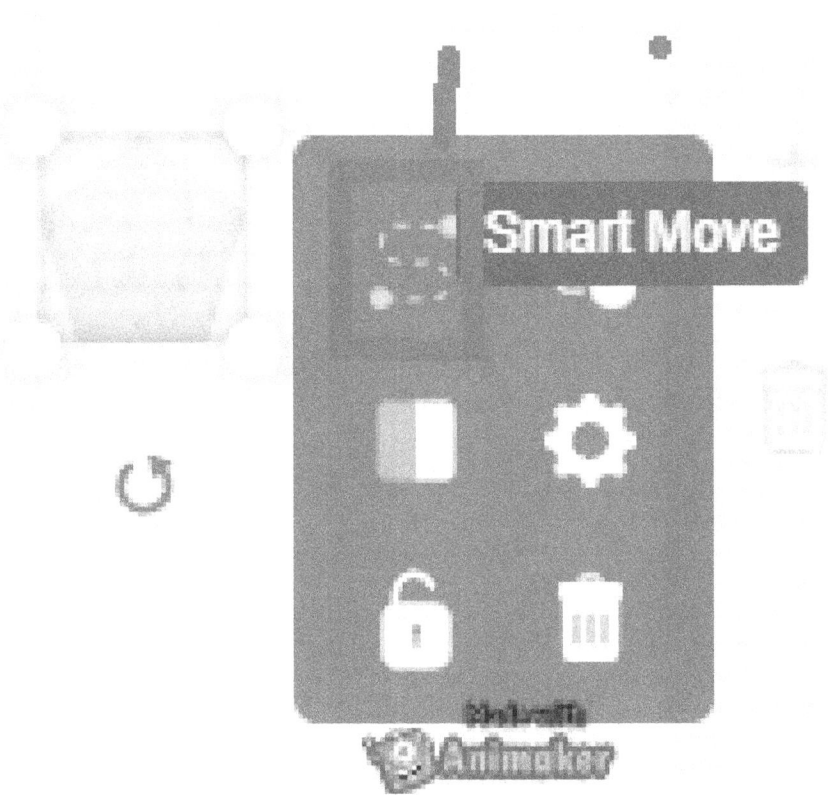

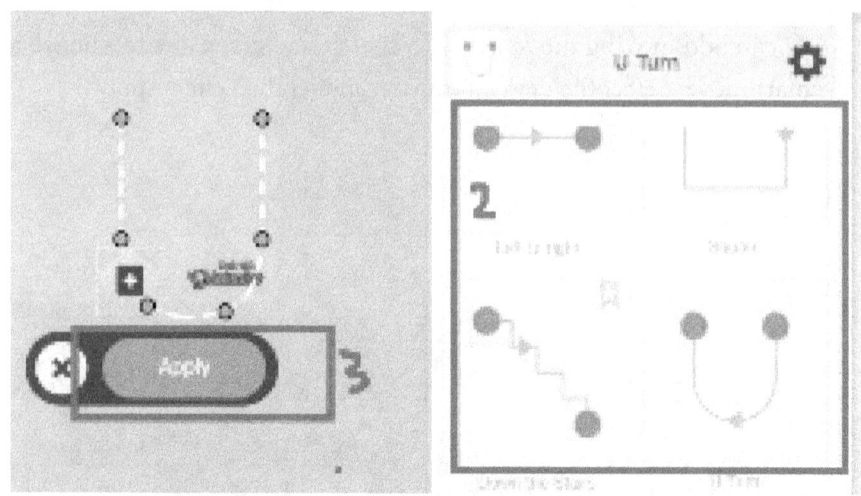

Flip, this menu is used to change or reverse the position of the shape. For example, face right, face left, up and down

PRACTICUM MODULE 3 (SHAPES)

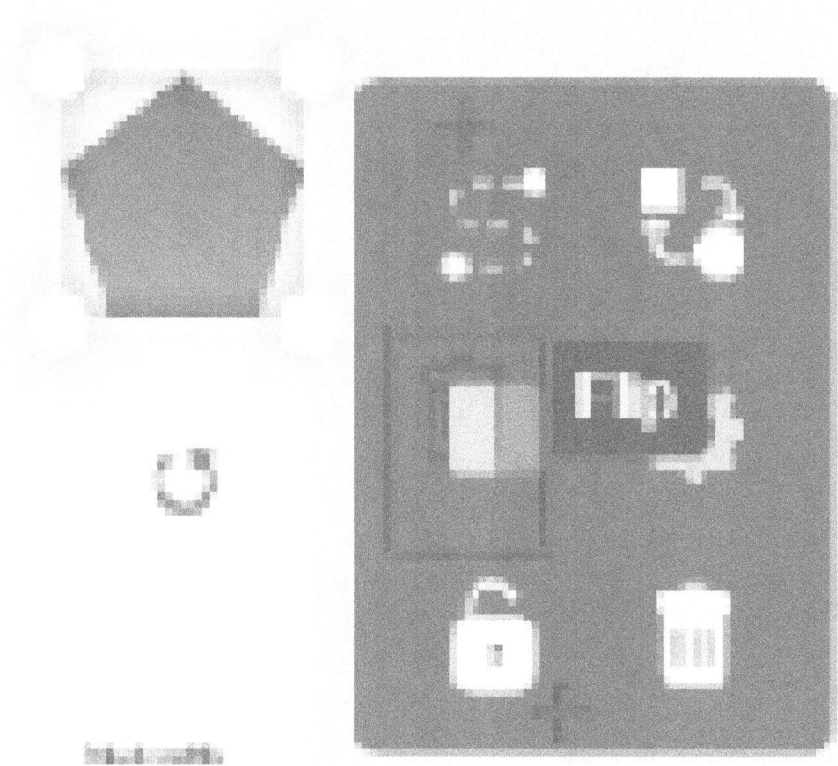

We can change the color of the shape. You do this by clicking the Settings symbol. We can change the color using custom themes, then add an enter and exit transition animation. We can also adjust the transparency of the shape

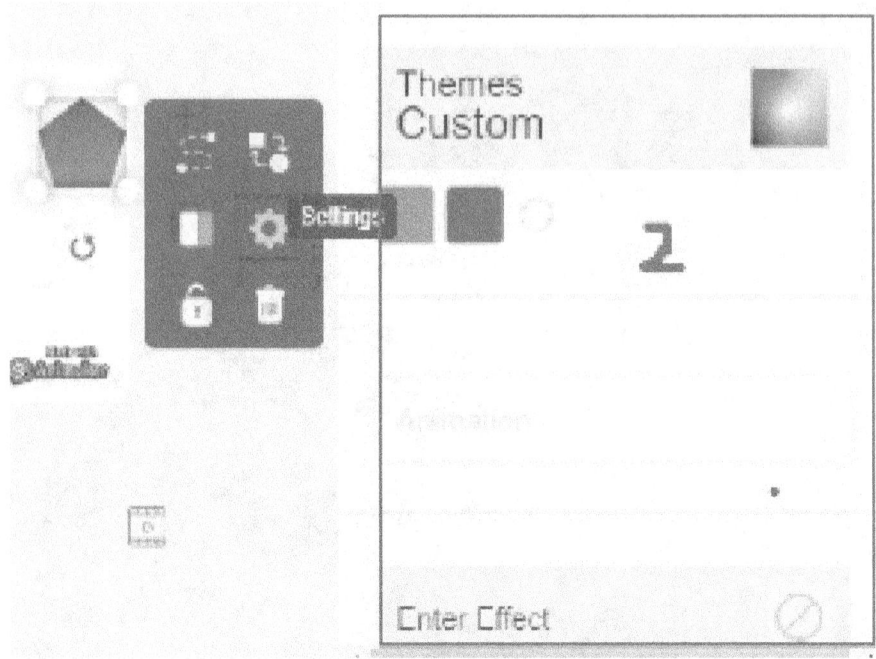

PRACTICUM MODULE 3 (SHAPES)

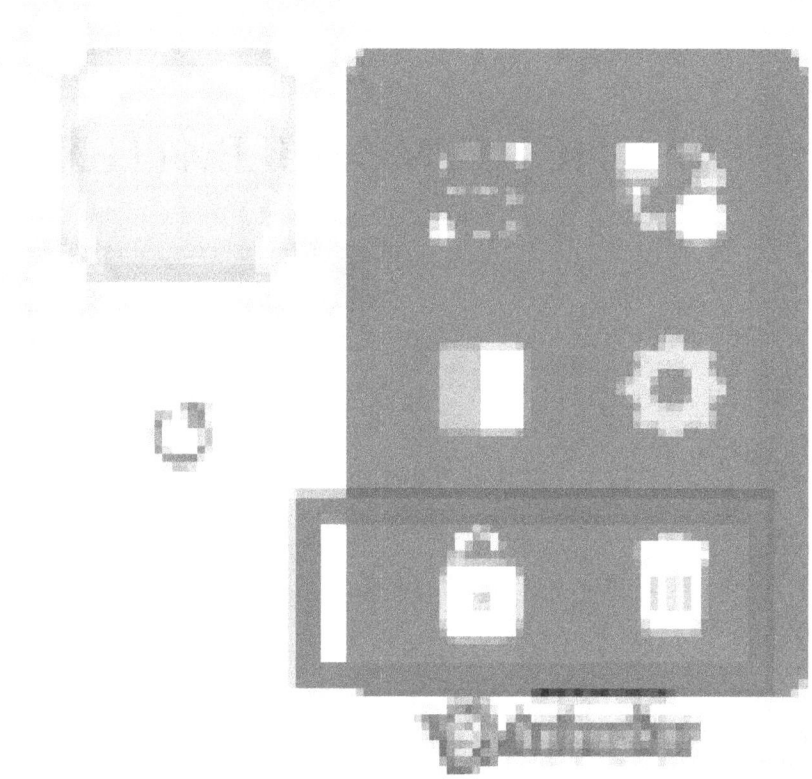

1. Lock, used to lock the shape so that it cannot be changed again. Trash is used to delete the shape

EVALUATION

1. What is meant by shape
2. Add 3 shapes to your project, then get creative with the three shapes by adding smart moves, then adjusting the colors and effects

PRACTICUM MODULE 4 (TEXT)

SUBJECT

- Text

LEARNING OBJECTIVES

- Students can understand and practice the use of text in animation i

DESCRIPTION

Text in animaker can be used as information, description or narration of an object.

TEST

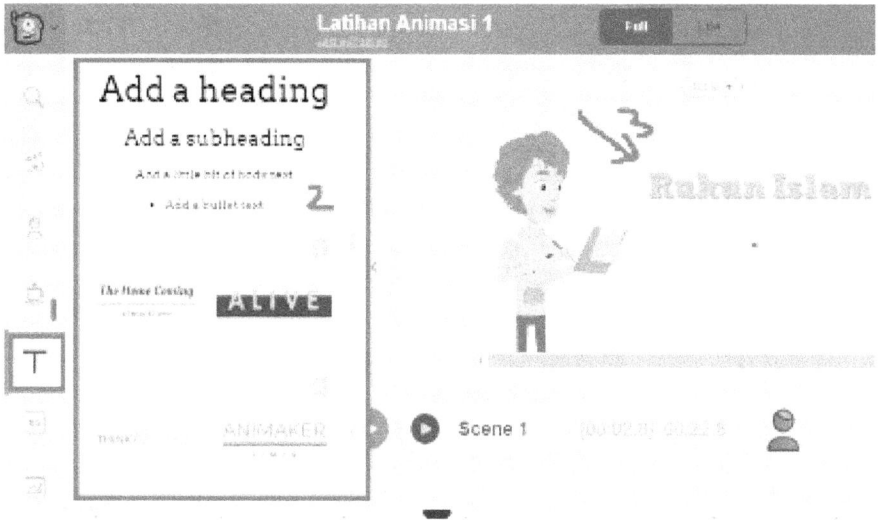

1. Select the menu with the T image on the left, then click on the text model you want. In this text section, there are many paid ones, but the free ones can also meet the needs for making animations.

PRACTICAL GUIDE TO IT-BASED INSTRUCTIONAL MEDIA DEVELOPMENT

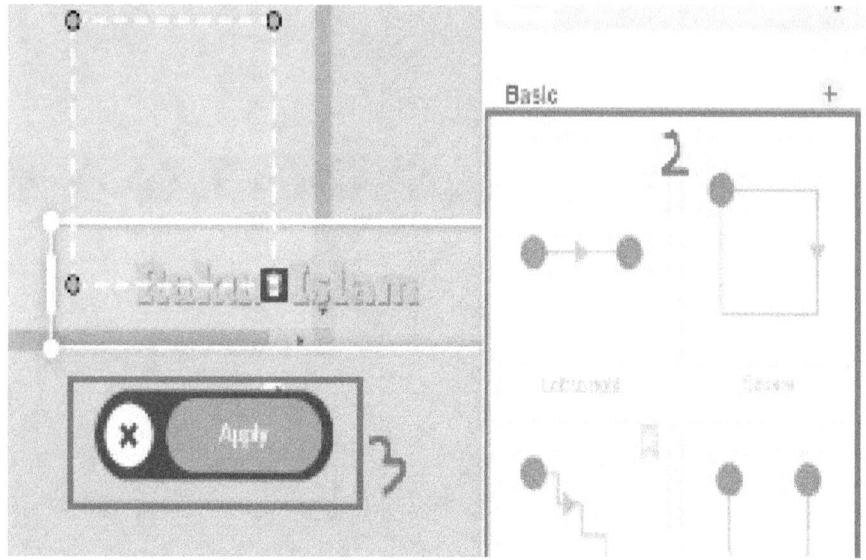

We can add moving movements to the text. How to choose a smart move. Select the desired displacement model then click

1. FX, used to give effects to text. The available effects are shadow (text shadow), offset, blur, and shadow models

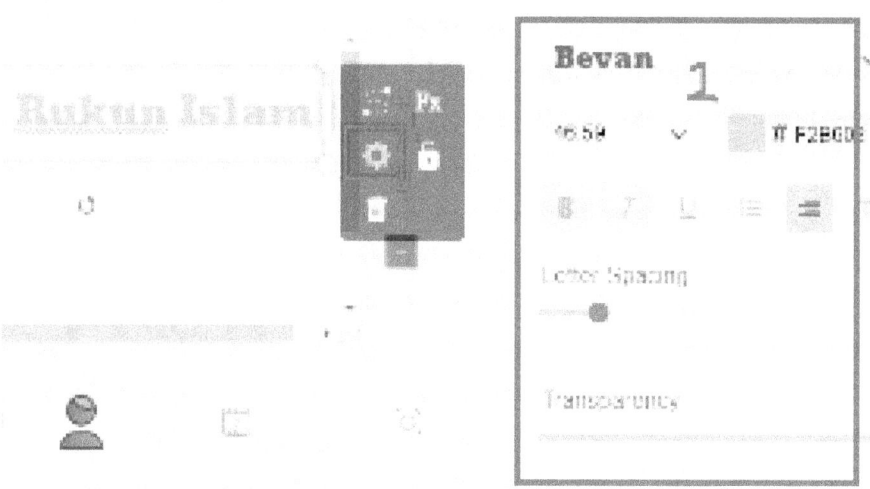

Click the Settings button to display the text settings. We can change text properties such as font type, size, color, margins, and so on. We can also add enter and exit transition animations. We can also adjust the transparency of the text

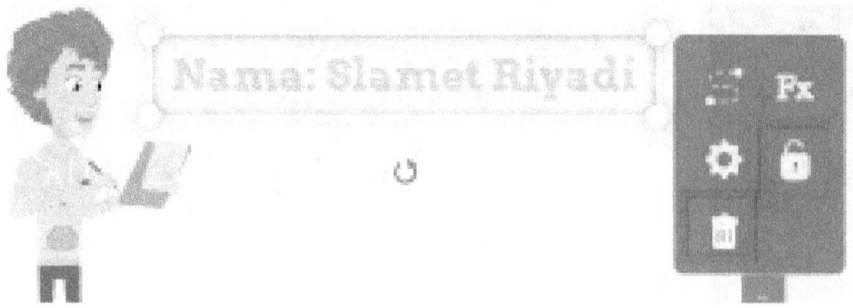

Lock, used to lock text so that it cannot be changed again. Trash is used to delete the text

EVALUATION

Add text to your project

Be as creative as possible with the text by adding movement, effects, coloring, and so on

PRACTICUM MODULE 5
(BACKGROUND)

SUBJECT

- Backgrounds

LEARNING OBJECTIVES

- Students can add backgrounds to projects

BASIC THEORY

Background is the background displayed in the video. Determining the right background is a very important process. Because this will describe the atmosphere in the animated video.

TEST

Select the menu with the BG image on the left, then click the desired background. In this background section, there are many paid ones, but the free ones can also meet the needs for making animations.

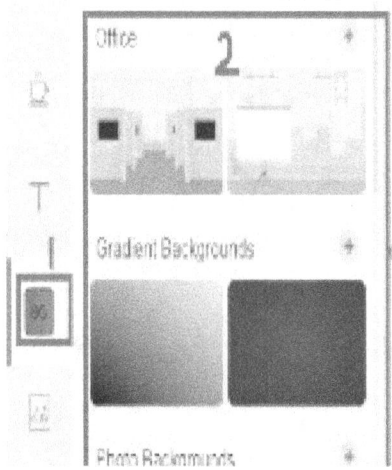 

The Filters button is used to display the effects that the background has. There are many options that can beautify the background. Click the desired effect option, then the background will change

 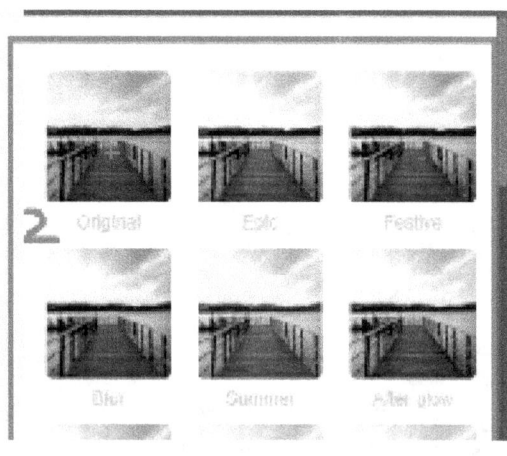

PRACTICUM MODULE 5 (BACKGROUND)

The Change Color button is used to change the background color. The steps are as in the picture beside this

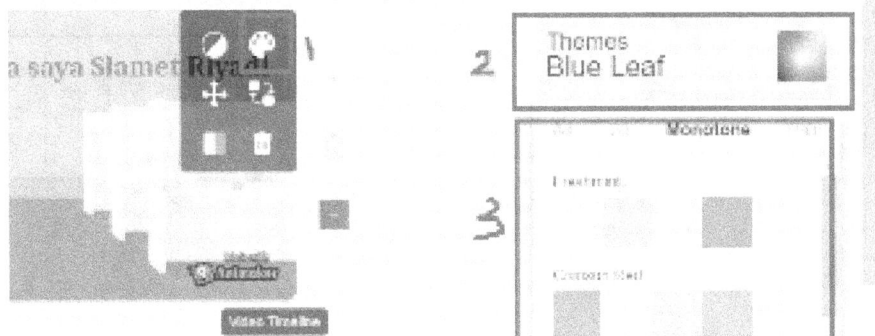

Click Resize to change the background size. Drag each corner to enlarge or reduce the background, then click Apply

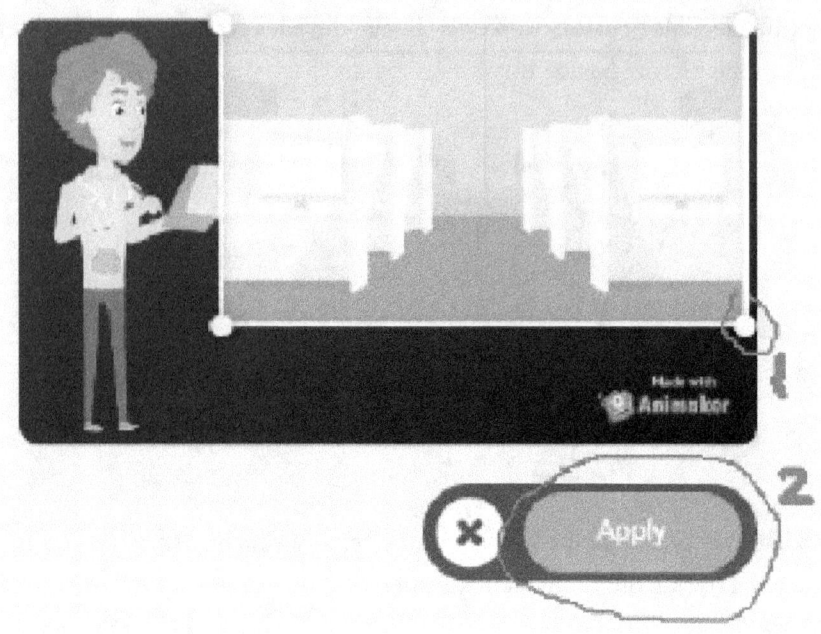

Flip, this menu is used to change or reverse the background position. For example, face right, face left, up and down. The Delete button is used to delete the background.

EVALUATION

1. Add a background to your project
2. Be as creative as possible with the background by changing the coloring, flip, and so on

PRACTICUM MODULE 6 (IMAGE, VIDEO, MUSIC)

SUBJECT

- Images, videos, music

LEARNING OBJECTIVES

- Students can add images, videos and music to the projects they have created
- Students can be creative by adding and arranging images, videos and music so that the animated videos they create are quite interesting.

BASIC THEORY

Image (English: image) is a combination of points, lines, planes and colors to create an imitation of an object – usually a physical object or human. Images can be in the form of two-dimensional images, such as paintings, photographs, or in three-dimensional form, such as statues.

Video comes from the Latin verb "videre to see", which was then used to create the new term "viddy", and was ultimately transformed into the word "video". According to Sukiman, video is a medium that can show images, accompanied by sound, and displayed at the same time. According to Cecep Kustandi, video is a tool that can explain processes, present information, teach skills, influence attitudes, shorten or slow down time, and explain complex concepts.

Music (Greek: μουσική, mousikê) is the art of arranging sounds or tones in such a way that they contain rhythm, song and harmony (KBBI). Music is a type of intuitive phenomenon, creating, improving and presenting it is a form of art (Marsela W., 2018).

TEST

To add an image, click the Image menu on the left. Then click on the desired image, it will be displayed on the screen/scene.

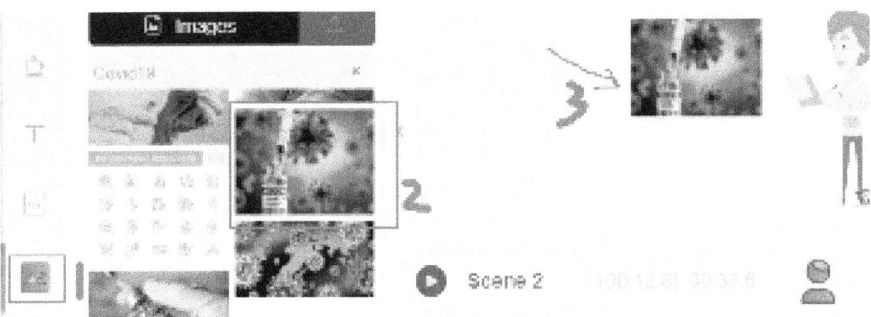

1. Click the Crop button to crop the image. The method is as in the picture beside. If it has been cropped, click Apply

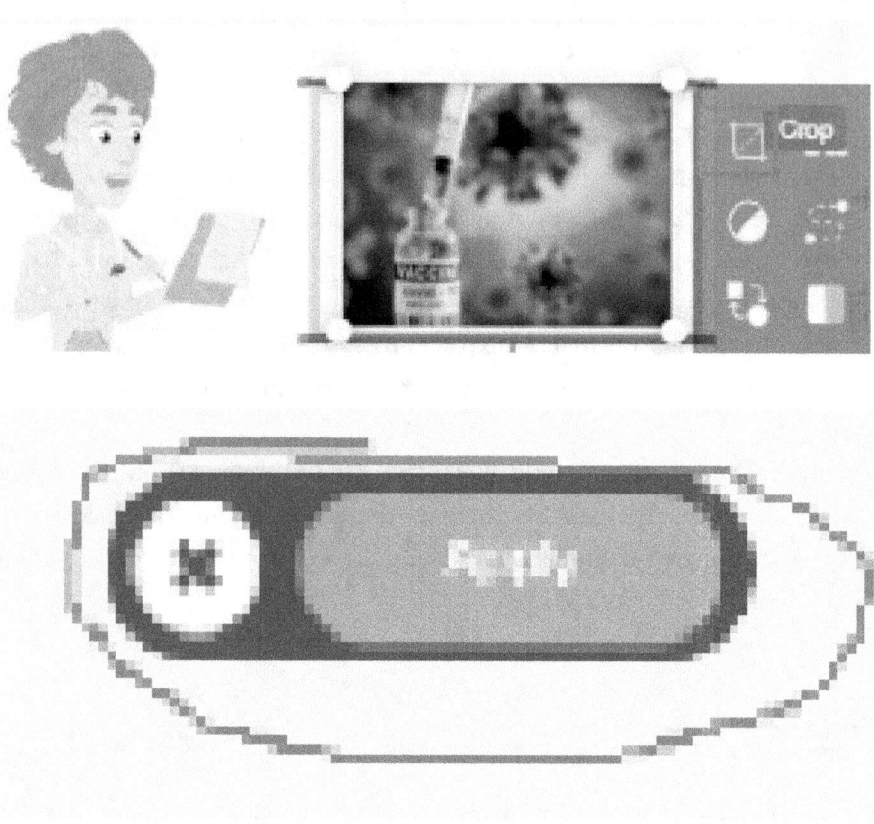

1. Filters are used to give effects to images. There are many choices of effects available

PRACTICUM MODULE 6 (IMAGE, VIDEO, MUSIC)

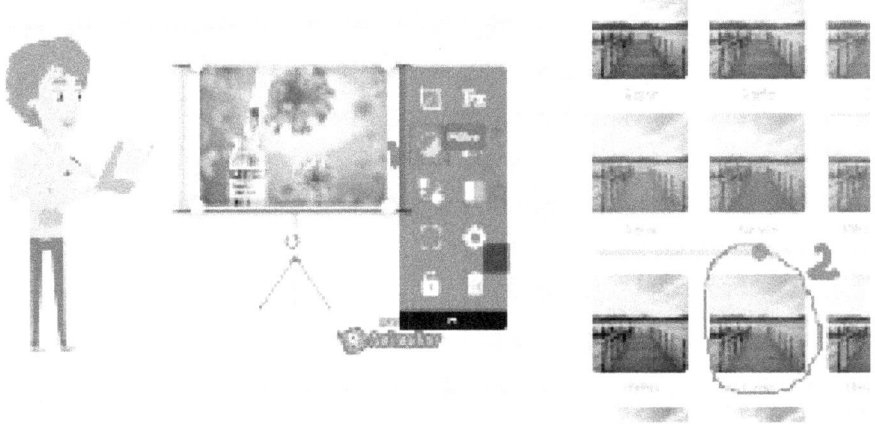

1. Apart from the 2 menus above, image also has other menus, namely

- Smart Move, movement to move places in the image
- Flip, this menu is used to change or reverse the image position
- Set as BG, sets the image as the background
- Settings, this menu is used to add enter effects (effects the first time the image is displayed), Exit effects (effects when the character has finished displaying), and Transparency (adjusts the transparency of the character

1. To add a video, click the video menu on the left. Then click on the video you want, it will be displayed on the screen/scene
2. The video also has property menus including

- Filters, used to give effects to videos. There are many choices of effects available
- Flip, this menu is used to change or reverse the position of the video
- Resize to change the video size

To add music, click the music menu on the left. Then click on the music you want, it will be displayed on the timeline/bottom. The music can be adjusted to sound from any second to any second

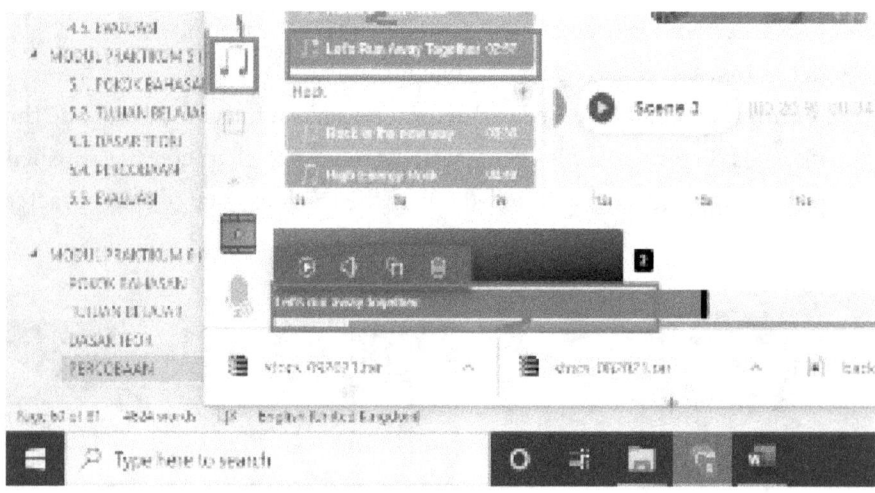

EVALUATION

1. Add images, videos and music to your project
2. Be as creative as possible with the images, videos and music by changing

the coloring, flipping and so on

PRACTICUM MODULE 7 (UPLOAD MENU)

SUBJECT

- Upload Menu

LEARNING OBJECTIVES

- Students can practice how to upload images, music and videos into the Animaker project

DESCRIPTION

PRACTICUM MODULE 7 (UPLOAD MENU)

Animaker provides a menu for uploading images, music and videos. Animaker provides 25GB of upload space. This space is certainly enough for us to use to upload supporting files for the animated video that will be created.

TEST

Click the upload menu in the left corner, then drag and drop the file to be uploaded into the space provided as in the image below. Wait until the upload process is complete.

The list of files that we uploaded will be displayed in My Files, as in the image beside. Drag the file into the scene page to insert it into the animated video

EVALUATION

1. Add image, music and video files to your project via the upload menu
2. Get creative with the images, videos and music you uploaded earlier by adding them to the scene page. Make it as interesting as possible by changing the coloring, flips, and so on

PRACTICUM MODULE 8 (SCENE AND TIMELINE)

SUBJECT

- Scenes
- Timeline

LEARNING OBJECTIVES

- Students can understand and practice the scenes and timelines in Animaker

BASIC THEORY

In the world of animation, the term scene is adopted as a container or place to collect scenes of similar panel images and frames. For example, when making a long animated story, it is really necessary to divide it into several scenes. Although using Scenes has several disadvantages, such as when we produce quite long animations.

If animation is the film, then the scene is the episode. With scenes we can arrange the order of scenes in the animation. This way it will be more organized, especially if it involves various menus and content jumps. Scenes are only there to make it easier for you to organize, no different from the others, we can cut, paste, etc.

Get used to using scenes for each different content in the animation, for example for the opening, body and ending. Scenes can be duplicated so that if we want several events that have the same sequence, but have different properties. We first create the base, then duplicate it, and apply the changes we want.

Timeline is a setting for the duration of a scene - the number of frames in a scene. Timeline can be used to organize and combine animations of various texts, images, audio and videos. The timeline in Animaker is divided into 3 parts which makes it easier for us to organize objects, video/audio, and camera.

TEST

To manage scenes, click the Scenes button at the top right. The scene list is displayed on the right. Select the scene that we want to set or make a video for, it will be displayed on the main screen.

PRACTICUM MODULE 8 (SCENE AND TIMELINE)

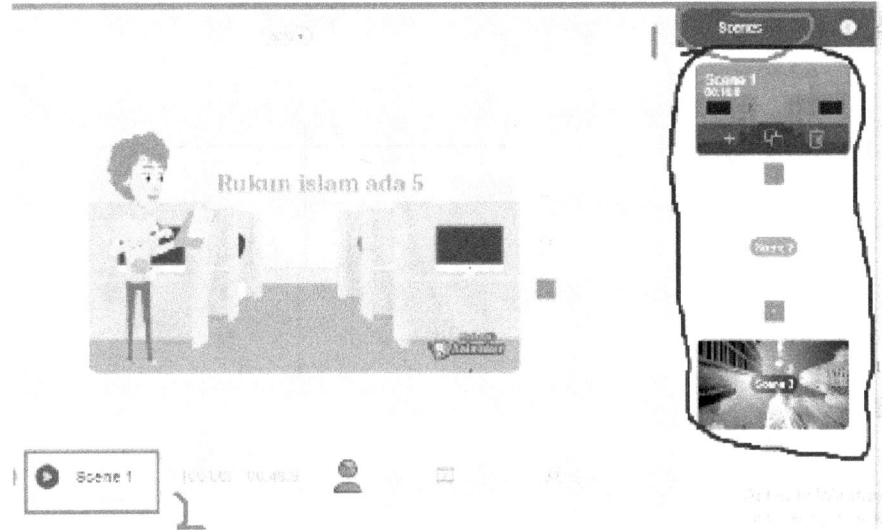

PRACTICAL GUIDE TO IT-BASED INSTRUCTIONAL MEDIA DEVELOPMENT

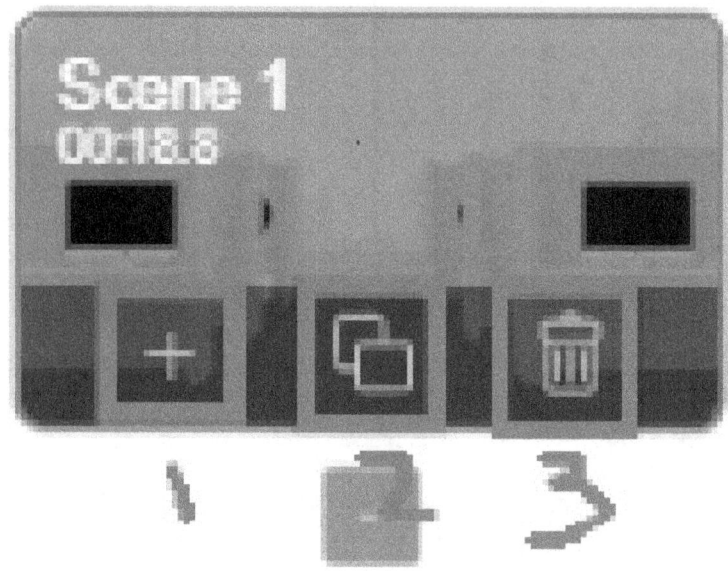

1. Each scene has an Add scene button (adds a new scene), Duplicate Scene (duplicates the scene), and Delete Scene (delete scene)
2. Timeline. Animaker divides the timeline into 3 parts, namely

3. Animation Timeline, used to control objects used in scenes such as characters, text and image

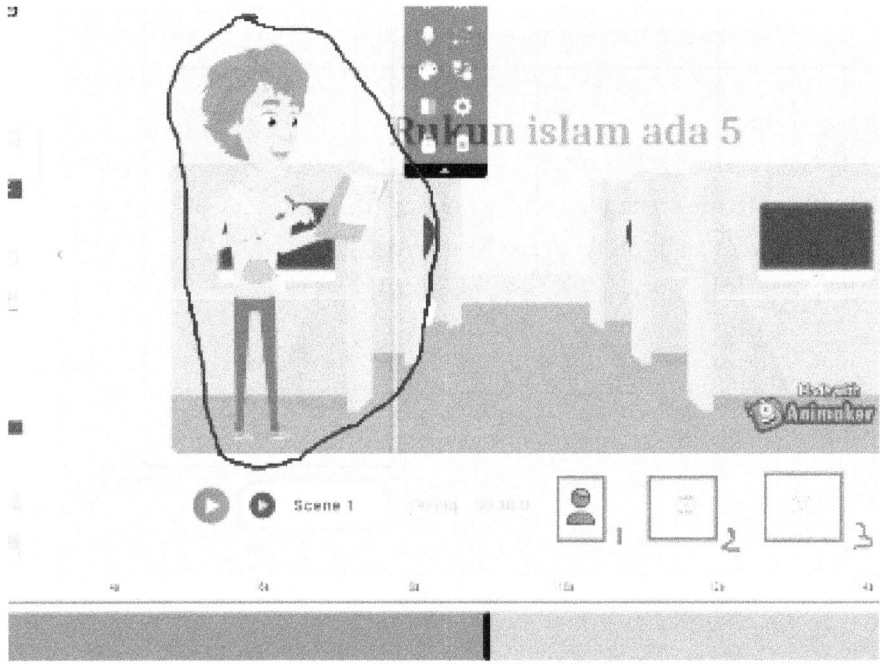

- Video/Audio Timeline, used to control the video/audio used in the scene
- Camera Timeline, used to control camera effects in the scene

For example, in the image above, to set a character, click on the animation timeline then click on the character, then at the bottom (marked in green) the timeline of that character will be displayed. In the timeline section, we can set which characters will be displayed from what second to what second

For video/audio timeline and camera timeline, the principle is the same as the animation timeline. We can set it to appear at what second to what second

EVALUATION

1. What is meant by scene in an animated video
2. Add a scene to your animaker project
3. Add characters, text, images, videos and music to the scene you just created
4. Get creative with characters, text, images, videos and music by adding them to the scene page and arranging the timeline in such a way that it produces an interesting animated video

PRACTICUM MODULE 9 (RENDERING)

SUBJECT

- Renderings

LEARNING OBJECTIVES

- Students understand and practice the rendering process in Animaker

BASIC THEORY

Rendering is a process containing steps to combine edited results in the form of objects in the form of photos, videos, audio, text, and so on.

The term Render or Rendering can be found in applications such as video editing applications, 3D applications, sound editing applications, and 2D applications. For example, when a user uses the 3D Sketchup application, at the modeling stage the building will look like a cartoon. New results will look real after rendering, such as shiny chairs, house buildings, and so on.

All activities regarding video are never separated from the rendering process. Without a rendering process, the video will not become a complete video. Before carrying out the rendering process, an editing process is usually carried out, namely by combining images, editing them, building them, until they become a single unit in the form of a video that depicts a story.

TEST

PRACTICUM MODULE 9 (RENDERING)

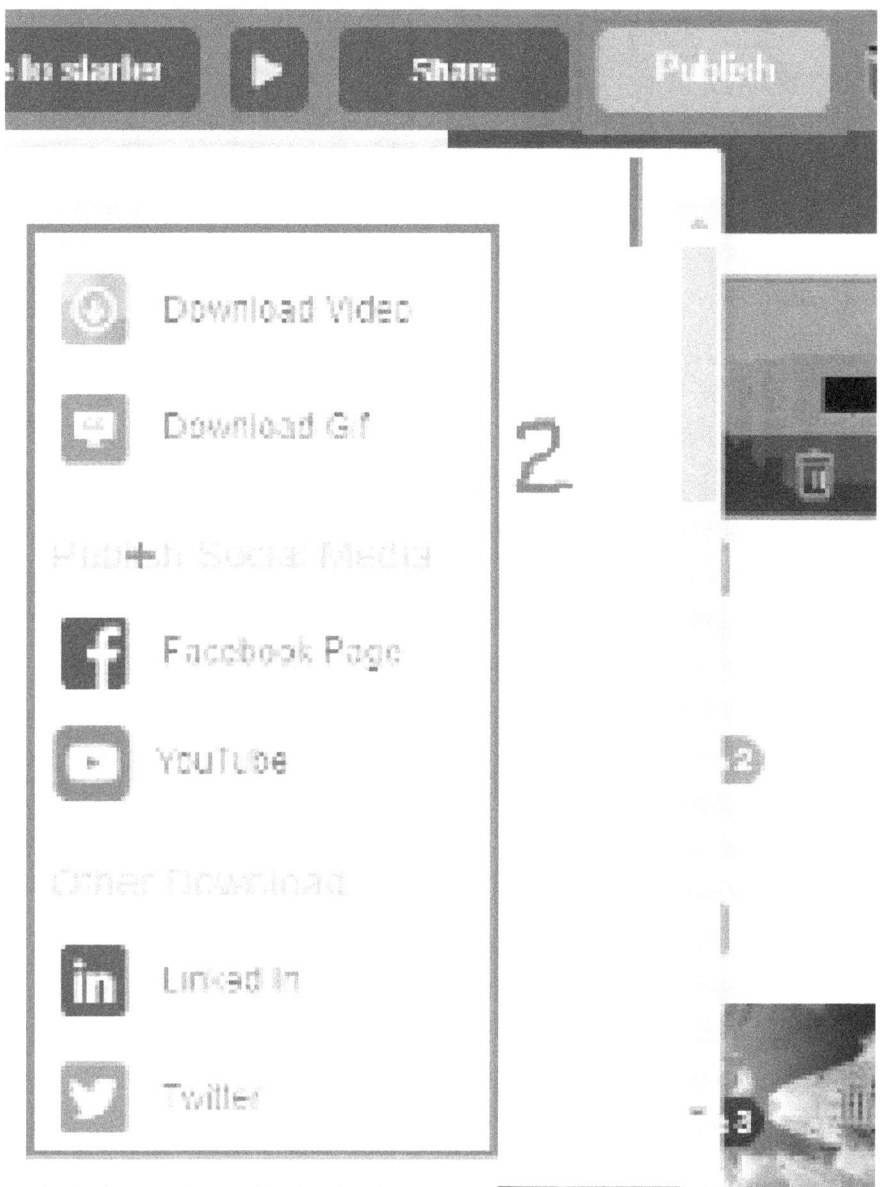

To start rendering, click the Publish button at the top right. There are many options displayed, whether we directly publish the rendering video on Facebook, YouTube, LinkedIn , and Twitter, a menu button is provided. If we only want to download the video, select Download Video.

PRACTICAL GUIDE TO IT-BASED INSTRUCTIONAL MEDIA DEVELOPMENT

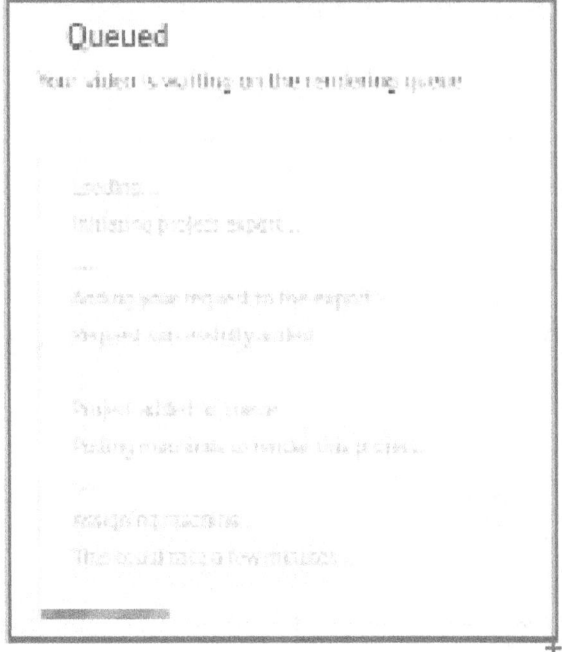

Next, the rendering process will be displayed. Wait for the process to complete.

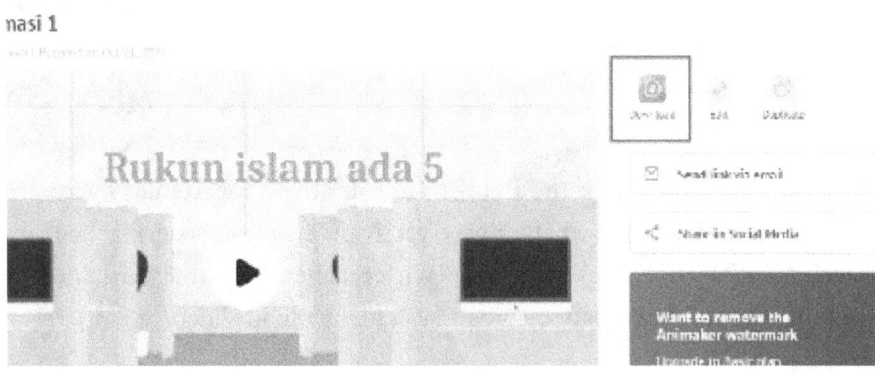

After the process is complete, the download page will be displayed. Click the download button on the right.

EVALUATION AND FINAL PROJECT

1. What is meant by scene rendering?
2. Create an IT-based learning media project using Animaker with a duration of 5 minutes! Be creative with this animaker to get media that is interesting for students, according to the age/class of the target students!
3. Run the rendering process of the project you have created in Animaker until it becomes a video file!

BIBLIOGRAPHY

1. Design Your Favorite Cartoon With Adobe Flash CS6, ISBN:978-979-29-3948-4, Medi Yanto, Andi Publisher, 2013.
2. Wahyuni, Sri. (2018). Development of Practical Modules for Basic Chemistry Courses on Reaction Rate Material at the Tarbiyah and Teacher Training Faculty of Uin ArRaniry. Banda Aceh: Uin Ar-Raniry Tarbiyah and Teacher Training Faculty.
3. Helianthusonrfri, Jefferly. (2019). Learn to Make Whiteboard Animation for Beginners. Jakarta: PT Elex Media Komputindo Gramedia Group.
4. Khoiriyah Mashuri, Delila. (2020). "Development of Volume Building Animation Video Learning Media for Class V Elementary Schools". JPGSD. Volume 08 Number 05.https://app.animaker.com/ , accessed 17 September 2021

ABOUT THE AUTHORS

S**lamet Riyadi, M.Kom** , born in Riau on 20 June 1986, is a Masters graduate in Informatics Engineering from STMIK AMIKOM Yogyakarta with extensive experience in developing and implementing information systems. He once worked as an IT Implementor at PT. Yogyakarta Software Application, IT Supervisor at Sampit Hospital, and Permanent Lecturer at Darwan Ali University. Apart from that, Slamet also has experience as an IT Programmer at PT. Sambu Island and as founder of CV. Daun Teknologi, working on various projects in government agencies and private companies. Slamet is also active in research, with several publications on application development, information systems and ERP technology. Special skills include web programming, desktop programming, database management, and networking. He is known as a professional who is responsible, dynamic, able to work in a team, and has good communication skills.

ABOUT THE AUTHORS

Dr. Hj. Rodhatul Jenna

, M.Pd, born in Martapura on 3 October 1967, is Dean of the Faculty of Tarbiyah and Teacher Training at IAIN Palangka Raya (2019-2023). He completed his education from SDN Tanjung Rema Martapura and earned a Strata 3 degree from Surabaya State University. He has extensive work experience, including Head of the Special Undergraduate Certification Program for GPAI, Head of the Education Laboratory, and Dean of FTIK IAIN Palangka Raya. Apart from that, he is active in various organizations such as Nasyiatul 'Aisyiyah and MUI. Dr. Rodhatul Jennah is also productive in research with many publications in leading journals, including research on the effectiveness of digital media and moral-based learning videos. He has written several books in the field of education and learning media development. His life motto is "No Day Without Achievement, No Achievement Without Hard Work.

www.ingramcontent.com/pod-product-compliance
Lightning Source LLC
Chambersburg PA
CBHW071957210526
45479CB00003B/969